D1143424

I didn't know that

giant pandas eat all day long

© Aladdin Books Ltd 2000
Produced by
Aladdin Books Ltd
28 Percy Street
London W1P 0LD

ISBN 0 7496 3422 7
First published in Great Britain in 2000 by
Aladdin Books/Watts Books
96 Leonard Street
London EC2A 4XD

Concept, editorial and design by

David West  Children's Books

Designer: Jennifer Skelly
Illustrators: Mike Atkinson, Jo Moore

Printed in Belgium

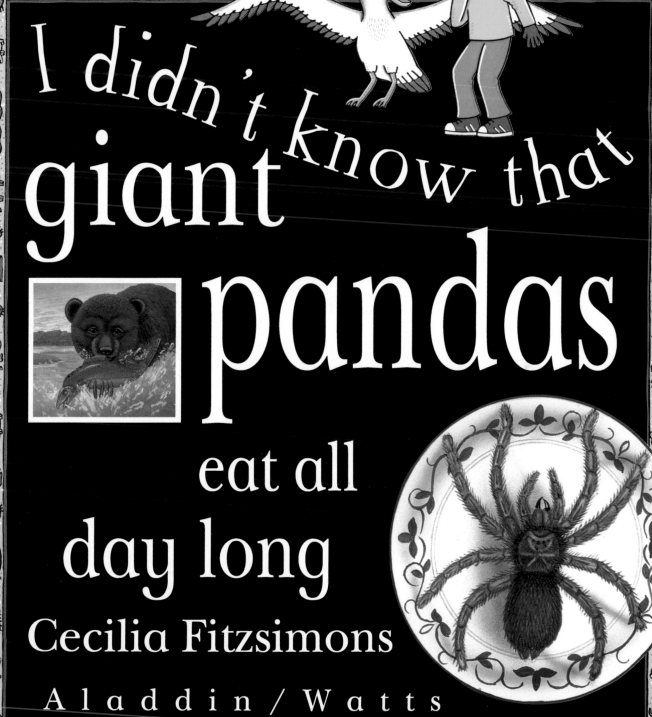

I didn't know that giant pandas

pandas

eat all
day long

Cecilia Fitzsimons

A l a d d i n / W a t t s
London • Sydney

I didn't know that

Introduction

Did *you* know that a harpy eagle can catch a monkey? ... that some big fish have wings?

Discover for yourself amazing facts about giant animals – just how big the biggest are, what they weigh, what they eat and much, much more.

 Look out for this symbol which means there is a fun project for you to try.

Is it true or is it false? Watch for this symbol and try to answer the question before reading on for the answer.

The giant clam can weigh up to 270 kg and grow up to one metre across.

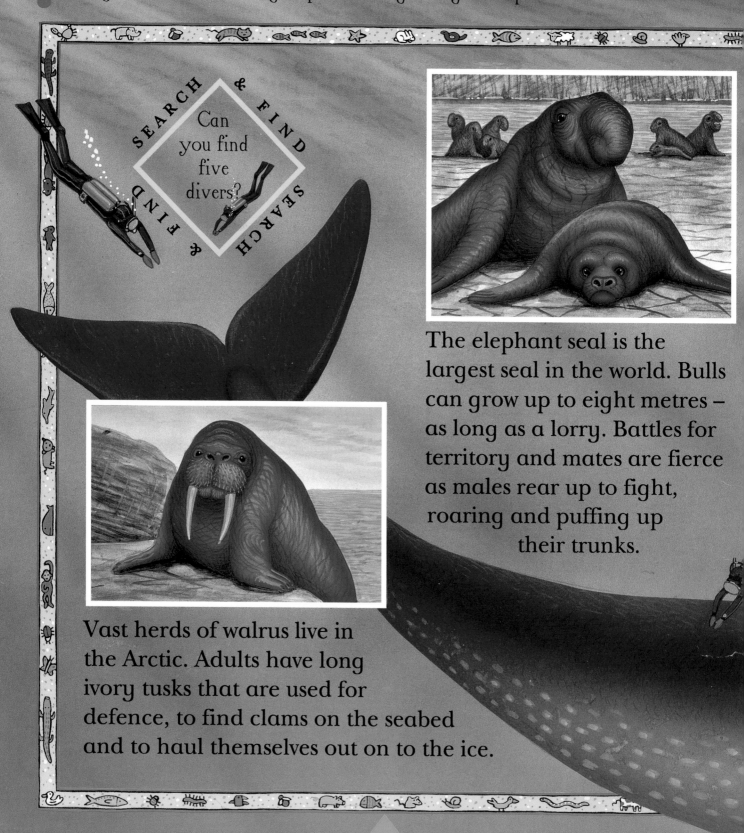

SEARCH & FIND SEARCH & FIND SEARCH

Can you find five divers?

The elephant seal is the largest seal in the world. Bulls can grow up to eight metres – as long as a lorry. Battles for territory and mates are fierce as males rear up to fight, roaring and puffing up their trunks.

Vast herds of walrus live in the Arctic. Adults have long ivory tusks that are used for defence, to find clams on the seabed and to haul themselves out on to the ice.

The dugong is a gentle giant with a short, whiskery muzzle. A flat tail like a mermaid's slowly propels the dugong through tropical coastal waters as it seeks banks of seaweed to graze.

I didn't know that

blue whales are the largest animals. They grow to 33 metres and weigh nearly 200 tonnes. This makes them the largest of all *mammals*, both in the sea and on land.

Blue whale

I didn't know that

the African elephant is the largest land animal. The biggest are four metres tall, over twice the height of the average human adult.

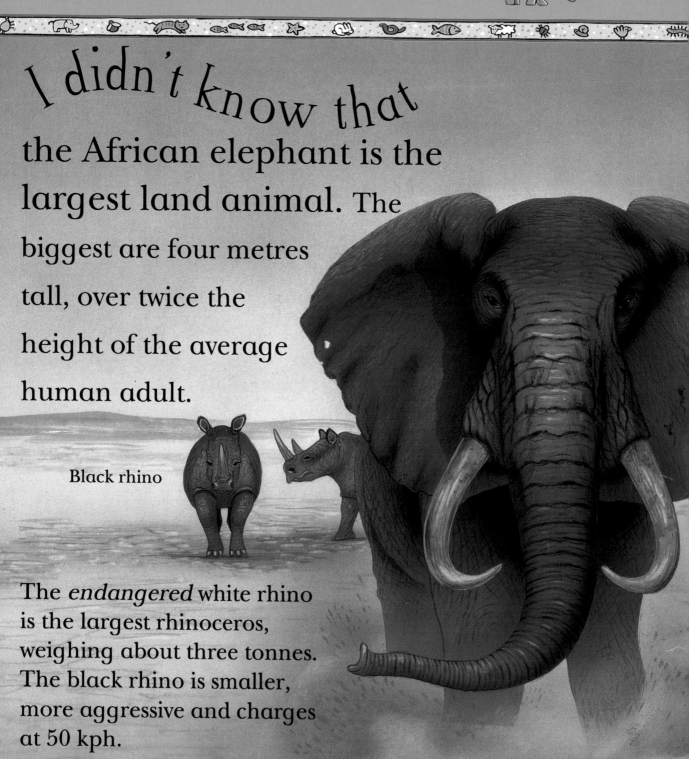

Black rhino

The *endangered* white rhino is the largest rhinoceros, weighing about three tonnes. The black rhino is smaller, more aggressive and charges at 50 kph.

Can you find three giraffes?

Giraffes are the tallest living animals. Five times as tall as you are, they can feed from the tree tops.

Hippopotamuses are heavy. Some weigh over three tonnes. They rest in rivers during the day, but feed on land at night.

An orangutan's arms can be up to three metres long from outstretched fingertip to fingertip. They use them to swing from branch to branch and to reach out for juicy fruit and leaves to eat.

Are you as heavy as a gorilla? Divide your weight into a gorilla's to find out how many of 'you' it would take to equal a gorilla's weight.

I didn't know that

gorillas can weigh over 180 kg. Most apes are large but gorillas are the largest *primates*. Even though they are slightly shorter than humans they weigh much more.

Can you find four baby gorillas?

SEARCH & FIND
FIND & SEARCH

I didn't know that

giant pandas eat all day long. They love bamboo. Bears, like pandas, have big appetites, some will hunt for meat or fish or they will eat insects and leaves.

Polar bears swim many kilometres across the icy Arctic seas. The tallest ever polar bear was three and a half metres tall!

Grizzly bears are excellent fishermen. When salmon *migrate* upstream to *spawn*, the bears arrive too. Wading into the fast-flowing rivers they scoop up fish with their paws.

 True or false?
Teddy bears are named after an American president.

Answer: **True**
The American president Theodore Roosevelt was nicknamed 'Teddy'. After he saved the life of a bear cub, shops began to sell 'teddy' bears.

I didn't know that

ostriches lay the biggest eggs. Each egg is 20 cm long and can weigh nearly two kilos. After they hatch, the chicks will live together in large flocks.

This is the size of an ostrich egg.

Swooping down through the rainforests of South America, the harpy eagle is the largest bird of prey. It can seize and fly away with howler monkeys and sloths that weigh more than five kilos.

Andean condor

Harpy eagle

The Andean condor soars over the Andes mountains in South America. With a *wingspan* of about three metres, these giant vultures feed on *carrion* as large as horses and cattle.

 True or false?
The albatross has the widest wingspan of all birds.

Answer: **True**
The wandering albatross that glides over the Southern oceans is the largest, with wings over three and a half metres across.

Some vultures eat so much that they cannot fly.

I didn't know that

Komodo dragons are the largest lizards. Only found on Komodo and nearby islands in Indonesia, the dragons grow to three metres in length and weigh up to 166 kg. They are one of many *species* of giant reptile.

Rare leatherback turtles can be almost three metres long. They live in temperate seas and eat jellyfish.

Saltwater crocodiles are the largest reptiles. Some grow to eight metres long and weigh over 500 kg. These dangerous man-eaters live in rivers, estuaries and the sea, from North Australia to South East Asia.

True or false?
Giant tortoises can live to be 150 years old.

Answer: **True**
A Seychelles tortoise was kept for 152 years on the island of Mauritius from 1766 until it died in 1918. It was probably about 200 years old.

The forest-dwelling reticulated python has been known to reach ten metres in length – the width of a tennis court. At night, it preys upon large animals, such as wild pigs, by crushing them within its body coils.

Anaconda

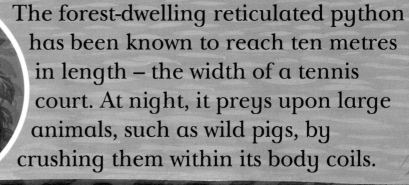

I didn't know that the anaconda is the heaviest snake. It lives in the swamps and rivers of South America and can grow to at least eight metres long and weigh more than 200 kg.

18

When disturbed, a cobra raises its head and spreads its flattened hood before striking. The king cobra is the largest and grows up to five and a half metres. Its bite can be fatal unless the victim is treated with *antivenom*.

Cobra

 True or false?

Gaboon vipers have the largest *fangs*.

Answer: **True**
The Gaboon viper lives in the forests of tropical Africa. Its poisonous fangs can be as long as your finger – about five centimetres!

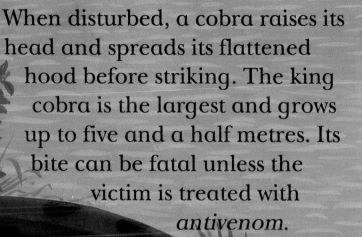

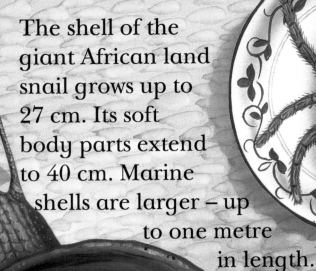

The shell of the giant African land snail grows up to 27 cm. Its soft body parts extend to 40 cm. Marine shells are larger – up to one metre in length.

The goliath bird-eating spider hunts in South America. It has a legspan of 28 cm – wider than a large dinner plate. Female spiders have bigger, heavier bodies than males.

You can measure some creatures. Cover the base of a plastic yoghurt pot with graph paper (one mm squares). Place an insect, spider or worm in the pot and measure it by counting the squares on the grid it covers.

Bootlace worms are very long. One measured 55 metres.

I didn't know that

the biggest butterfly is this big! The Queen Alexandra's birdwing butterfly lives in the forests of New Guinea. It has a wingspan of 28 centimetres. It is a rare and endangered species.

The heaviest beetle is the goliath beetle, a type of *scarab* from tropical Africa. Only 11 cm long, its heavy body may weigh 100 g. The South American hercules beetle is longer but lighter.

I didn't know that

some fish have wings. Manta rays gently flap their wide, wing-like fins in warm, surface waters, sometimes leaping from the water as if in flight.

Massive ocean sunfish float in the surface currents of the oceans. Over four metres long, they seem to be all head, with no body or tail.

Sunfish

True or false? Giant squid's eyes are bigger than basketballs.

Answer: **True**
Little is known about these mysterious animals. One of the largest found had eyes that were 40 cm across – the size of a car tyre!

The tropical whale shark is the biggest fish at 13 metres long. Like basking sharks and whales it feeds on *plankton*.

Whale shark

23

I didn't know that

goliath frogs can weigh more than 3.6 kg. These giant frogs from West Africa are 30 cm long, or 87 cm with their legs stretched out! North American bullfrogs live in rivers, lakes and ponds. They can grow to a similar size, but are not as heavy.

South American cane toads were released in Australia to eat insect pests. Now there are too many toads there.

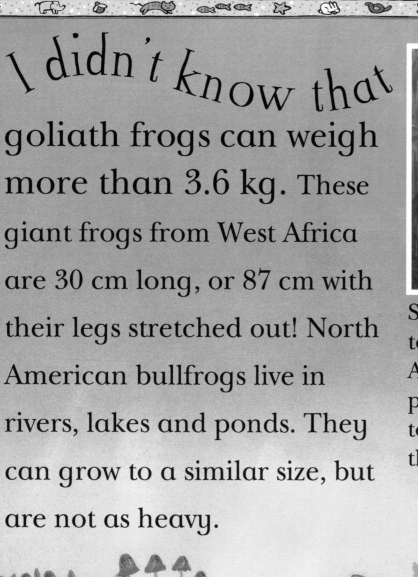

Japanese and Chinese giant salamanders are the largest amphibians alive today. Living in the bottom of cold mountain rivers, they can grow to 1.8 metres in length.

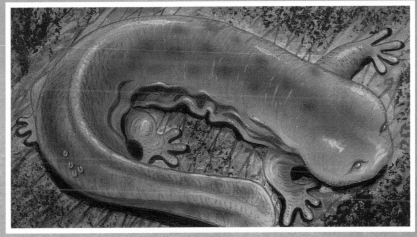

Goliath frog

 True or false?
Toads lay more eggs than any other animal.

Answer: **False**
Cane toads may lay up to 35,000 eggs, but many fish also lay vast numbers of eggs. The ocean sunfish lays at least 300 million eggs.

With an awesome wingspan of 15 m, Quetzalcoatlus was the largest flying animal. In flight these *pterosaurs* were as large as a small plane.

True or false?
Megalodon was the largest prehistoric shark.

Answer: **True**

Only Megalodon's teeth remain, but these tell us that the fish was like a huge great white shark. It was probably 13 metres long. The whale shark today is about the same size.

Megalodon's tooth

Ultrasaurus

After the dinosaurs died out the most ferocious carnivores were enormous flightless birds. Diatryma was three metres tall, with strong legs, claws and a massive, meat-tearing beak. It preyed on small mammals.

Diatryma

I didn't know that sauropods were the biggest animals to have walked the Earth. Only a few remains have been found. The largest ones belong to a long-necked dinosaur 18 metres high. Taller than a four-storey building a human would have barely reached its ankles!

Prehistoric man built huts with five-metre-long mammoth tusks.

I didn't know that

we were so small. Yet no other animal has had such an effect on the Earth's creatures. By hunting and by destroying *habitats* we have brought some species close to extinction. The natural world with all of its plants and animals needs our protection to survive.

Bird-eating spider

Grizzly bear

Gorilla

African elephant

Saltwater crocodile

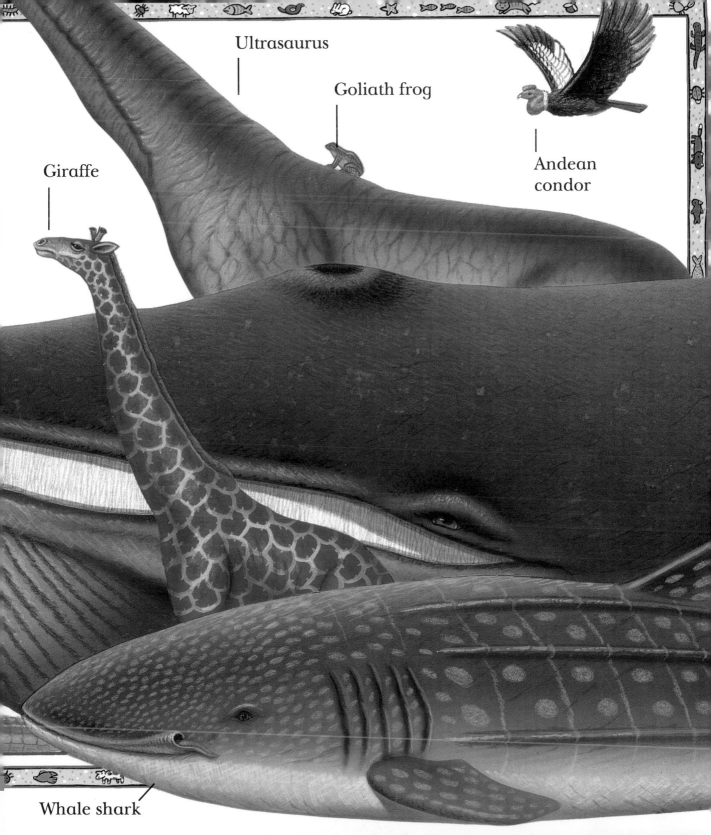

Ultrasaurus

Goliath frog

Andean
condor

Giraffe

Whale shark

Glossary

Antivenom
A medicine used to treat the venom (poison) from bites inflicted by snakes and other poisonous animals.

Carrion
Meat from a dead and often rotting animal that was previously killed by a predator, or died by accident or by natural causes.

Endangered
An animal or plant that is so rare, that unless both it and its habitat are protected, it will become extinct.

Fang
A long pointed tooth. Snakes use their hollow fangs to inject venom into their victims.

Habitat
The natural surroundings or home of an animal or plant.

Mammal
An animal such as a shrew that gives birth to live young that it feeds on milk.

Migrate
Long distance travel by animals from one place to another, usually to breed.

Plankton

Small animals and plants that live by floating in the sea or freshwater.

Primate

A member of the primate family, which includes humans, apes and monkeys.

Pterosaurs

A group of flying reptiles that lived during the age of dinosaurs.

Sauropods

Enormous plant-eating dinosaurs, with elephant-like bodies and incredibly long necks and tails.

Scarab

Dung beetles; they collect animal dung and lay their eggs in it.

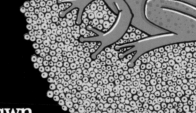

Spawn

To lay vast numbers of eggs.

Species

A type of animal or plant.

Wingspan

The distance between the tips of a pair of outstretched wings.

Index